FINE

MATT RADER

FINE

NIGHTWOOD EDITIONS

Nightwood Editions
P.O. Box 1779
Gibsons, BC VON 1V0
Canada
www.nightwoodeditions.com

COVER DESIGN: Myron Campbell
TYPOGRAPHY: Libris Simas Ferraz / Onça Publishing

Nightwood Editions acknowledges the support of the Canada Council for the Arts, the
Government of Canada, and the Province of British Columbia through the BC Arts Council.

This book has been printed on 100% post-consumer recycled paper.
Printed and bound in Canada.

LIBRARY AND ARCHIVES CANADA CATALOGUING IN PUBLICATION
Title: Fine / Matt Rader.
Names: Rader, Matt, 1978- author.
Description: Poems.
Identifiers: Canadiana (print) 20230574831 | Canadiana (ebook) 20230620671 |
    ISBN 9780889714663 (softcover) | ISBN 9780889714670 (EPUB)
Subjects: LCGFT: Poetry.
Classification: LCC PS8585.A2825 F56 2024 | DDC C811/.6—dc23

For Nancy & Sharon

no mistake

between every line

a lake

Table of Contents

Fine

Where I lived there were still grasslands

but very few

between the condos

and roadways

and subdivisions. The grasses

my friend said

were fire

in its low entropy state

but fire

was no kind

of grass. I wanted to say something back then

about the synonyms

territory / state / condition

I wanted to make a shift from *fire* to *fine*

its averageness, its elegance

its penalty

Then the helicopters lifted the cold dark energy of the lake

into the sky

like a chalice

There was an icon on my phone that looked like a face

disguised by smoke

There were masks that helped us breathe

by restricting our breathing

There were evenings of no smoke

when we could see for ages across the valley

through all time

Our medicine was medicine and walking

among the drought-stricken yellow cedars, seeing the bodies

of people moving through water

especially women

which even then stirred me

also men

also not everything

had definition, like smoke, fantasies

a third thing I felt

too shy to mention. I'd always wanted

to be funnier than I was

but verily we laughed

looking for our phones which we were clutching

looking at pictures

of our hair

In those days we grew tomatoes so sweet and deformed

we called them *care*

We were aware

of a shape we could not regard directly

lurking at the centre of things

We will have been that shape is all we could say truthfully

about what we knew

With our hands we could swim

in the museum

through screens of digital modelling

unthickened time

to see the city

before the city, its reeds and waterways, the white outline

spectre of buildings

hovering above everything

the future anterior

what we were

what we will have been

Working on My Brother's Farm in Errington, BC

My brother didn't speak

until he was five

Didn't read

or write

until twelve

I'm writing this

in the lee of my truck

on our midday break

in a field of yellow asters

There are parts of this story that can't be told

without hurting someone

How to listen

to silence

from within

silence. My brother's

two-year-old son

holding my hand, pointing

at flowers and trucks

When we read

a silence

we change it. I can't tell you

what it's like

to be outside

language

inside language. The tall grass

at the edge

of the field makes shapes

in the breeze

My brother walking open

the big aluminum gate

The metallic-blue

damselfly

nodding on my knee

Guests, Syilx Territory

for Peter Morin

RUSSIAN OLIVES

On my slow journey upriver

between two orchards

I saw a delta of Russian olives

Most of the water in that valley

flowed across the sky

but from the dry earth

the Russian olives drew

fantastic silver-blue tributaries

that floated in the wind

waving as I passed

They were the colour

of your mother's hair

and I could see you brushing them

and braiding them

a kind of remembering

not all things that come are invited

not all uninvited things go

We live on

water and light and gravity

The rivers are waving as they pass

but not at us

Beyond the waters of the oleaster

a dark wood grows

ITALIAN OLIVES

Once in a time of fire

we shared a small white bowl

of Italian olives

that had travelled a long way

to be with us

on the high plateau

in the valley of the ancient lake

Smoke made of the city

a dim, orange afterworld

forgetting first

the sky, then

the mountains, then

the buildings

across the street

We held the deep green orbs

between our fingers

like the eyes of fish. In their flesh

I tasted the heat and brine

of a distant land

a distant sea

My mother's family

came from that land, that sea

Some pits are an emptiness

others a truth

There's a hardness

from which olives grow

Heat Dome

We swam in the lake at 9 am

before it grew too hot

to be

outside

the five of us

two divorced parents

our teenagers

my mother

at the little public access

next to the stone manor with tennis courts

and lakeside infinity pool

I had a spider bite

on my hip

the exact pinks of the wildfire

smoke-filtered

sunlight. In Keremeos and Osoyoos and Penticton

the ashes of Catholic churches

can't cool

Spider-bite sky

Rashy light

In Xanadu, did Kubla Khan

A stately pleasure-dome decree

is what I remember

most vividly from grade 12 poetry

Infinity is when

it never ends. We swam out

to the nearest buoy

a white and pink ball on the surface

of the lake. We followed its shadowy chain down

to a shadowy slab of concrete

in the milfoil at fifteen feet

What is pleasure

without an ending

When the spider bit me

I didn't feel anything. Back on the beach

on our slip of public property

beneath a bower of maple trees

we were cool. How could we be

happy, we asked

but we were

happy. The spider bite had its own source

of heat. It was something

inside me

Cactus + Cigarette + Unicorn

for Neela

The prickly pear is *Real*

you say

especially its rays

of calcified light

we might toothpick

our current feelings with

What gives?

If I spit

on the dry biotic crust

of the desert

with its twenty-seven varieties

of vegetation

it turns a bright red

Desert indicators include

the darkling beetle

and antelope brush

The desert is what you get

when you get less

and *Less*

plus bunchgrass

A cigarette

followed by a unicorn head

is what I text friends

to express *Rare Pleasure*

In my mind

I pick a memory

of a crisp summer beach

on the Salish Sea

the sea itself

frenzied

by pins of light

This is where I go

when I want to be alone

and happy

inside my body

In its dormant stage

the prickly pear resembles

a sore thumb

with acupuncture added

But the prickly pear

is green now, plump

almost ready

to abracadabra

its yellow

handkerchief of bloom

Selfie

Out beyond the cadet base firing range

the sea was orgasmic, blinding, totally insane

the heavy pixelated water

the pixelated sand

our bodies pixelated

shredded completely by unfathomable quanta

We didn't exist yet

as we'd come to exist, pure data, light packets

I could still touch things

like the beach face

like the brilliant, shattered sea

I had hands, feet, hair on my arms and between my legs

I was a man

My skin was coriander and salt

Ultraviolet radiation

was already transforming me

replicating genetic material in my body

at alarming rates

I'd misread *motion recollected in tranquility*

I knew that time

was a product of heat, things cooling eventually

a kind of poem

with a tail

personal history

I was raised on an island

at the western shore of an industrialized nation

in the last decades

of the twentieth century

I can go there even now

through a trapdoor

in the mirror

of my memory

a font of plovers

texting themselves across low water

the tideline refreshing itself continuously

pure impulse

pure signal

I was white in a midden of white things

I was myself finally just as a self was something

we might cease to be

Hot Winter

Not just her marigold bikini

and its pools

of flesh

but the dark amber river pool

she slipped into

its deep

shadows, its slick bronzed rocks

its coolness

in the burnt, cedar-filtered

afterlight

of whatever comes next. Light slows

in wildsmoke

and bends

the mind

toward futures. To meet abandonment

with abandon

is one idea. Sandstone and honey sky

Someone's wife

swims through the darkness

before me

goldenrod skin

burning

pine

air. I want

new ideas, badly

I want to be the lichened rock in winter

licked by low sun

feeding

meltwater nitrogen

to my gravity

shadow

a mute

pool of unswimmable density

hot hot winter

Not just

the self-healing

human-shaped wound the water arranges

and rearranges

in itself

as she moves

but the ash

swirling in smokelight

Blue-Eyed Mary

Days when the only ethic

is clarity. To know

where you are

under a titanium sky. To say I hurt

people I love

people. The names of flowers

are only our names

for flowers

tiny blue-lipped

white-of-the-eye petals

eating the sun

Autocorrect

I came to give thanks

that autumn weekend in the Canadian desert

tawny light

blue sky against sage

The north wind kept shoving the lake

towards the US border

whitecaps

stumbling like prisoners

autocorrected

back to lake water. That's what the mind does

distract itself

invent things. I went for a run

to where a point of land

reaches out like predictive text across the lake

almost to the other side

file name: anarchistmountain.jpeg

file name: sẃiẃs.mp3

A small yellow rain

of light dripped

from the peachleaf willows

along the shore. They were so wet

it was almost obscene

I felt hot

in the sun. In tree shadow, flesh rising on my arms

like an old memory. I can't remember

any jokes I told

my daughters

for sixteen years before bed

just the laughter

is what I thought, running out

along swiẃs toward the opposite shore

Imagine how stressful it would be

to remember everything

Imagine your disappointment

I said to myself, as a gate

into some meadow

estates you've avoided until today

At home after the run

I felt sad. I wrote in my diarrhea. Fuck. Dairy. Fuck

Then I was laughing

still feeling sad. Those prisoners out on the lake

the border. Sadness is free

floating. I held down the space bar

and moved the cursor

into the antelope brush and big sage

where a little tuft of desert buckwheat grew

like a cowlick on the dark rocks

their many swatches of lichen

pale green, lime green, copper rust

Someone's femur on the desert's dry biotic crust

bone-white bone

like a virgule

among the golden rabbitbrush. Don't end on an easy image

file, portable network graphic

Nothing you can do

will save you or anyone else

from death

yet

look at this

Pineappleweed

Sometimes I think

we make too much

of form. Maybe intuition

is really unspoken

desire, the sudden

wordless

recognition of

a pattern

we'd wanted

so recognized. Crushed

pineappleweed

tastes like pineapple

if you say the name

pineappleweed

before you taste it

After your illness

they wrapped

your prosthetic

breasts in the skin

of a cadaver. A living

human body

they said

prefers human death

to polymers

The tiny yellow buds

of pineappleweed

look like pineapples

without skins

if you want them to

When you had them

remove

the implants

you became more

yourself again

Atmospheric Moon River

December loomed

with its supply chain of moods

The plum tree's last medallions of golden leaves

its rivière of blue

light emitting diodes for Diwali

In my dreams

I could do no violence. No matter how

hard I tried

I had no force to execute my attacks

I stomped

dream body after dream body

but no one

was ever hurt

as if something wanted

to remind me, even in my sleep

of my impotence

in global affairs, as if something wanted

to save me. *Westron wynde when wyll thow blow*

I listened

to *In a Sentimental Mood*

nightly. I borrowed a distinction between porn

and pornography

Mornings, the moon lowered itself

over the western mountains

and hung there

golden white

against the sky's cool complexion

not even looking at me

but looking at me

if you know what I mean

Tomorrow sex will be good again

is a phrase I read

and repeated via text to a colleague

working on affect theory

in Hungary

a person

for whom I had indeterminate feelings

Psychic excess

they called it

quoting

Judith Butler Yeats

On the other side of the mountains

a thin river of water

poured like grief through the atmosphere

wiping out everything

bridges, hillsides, farmland

Only debt survived

barely

I got to thinking

how that cameo moon might look on me

with my undertones

of firebush and raspberry

my cobalt

disbelief in money

the thin tremulous needle of futurity

that fluttered

in all my poetry. I was in an elevator

ascending a glass tower

the floor numbers lighting up

like cigarettes

in the dark, like parts of my brain

when I sang

the *smalle rayne downe can Rayne.* Across the province

we gathered

candles and sandbags

We prepared

to lose all

power

Above the building

beyond the many panels of tempered glass

a tower crane floated

in the river

of rain. Even then we knew abundance

Autumn's harvest

of darkness

in which tiny green lights grew

like mushrooms

along the jib of the crane

Cryst yf my love were in my Armys

And I yn my bed Agayne

I heard

the wind sing

There's no such thing

as an aesthetic death mudslide

Atmospheric moon river

I'm crossing you

Sweet Air

You don't hear anymore

in your sleep

the continental night trains

their congested iron engines wheezing

in the sidings along the lake

a couple hundred feet

from your apartment window

But when I sleep

in your bed, I still wake in the night

feeling shunted

away from myself

as if an element of my subconscious

metallic, impenetrable

loaded with ore and minerals

were travelling

without me

through the dark mountains

toward the industrial seaports on the Salish coast

Last summer in Sunnybrae

we watched from across the lake

a kilometre of railcars

the colour of old memories

slowly describe the shoreline westbound

below Mount Tappen

What are they hauling? I asked, knowing

we didn't have an answer

The insides of mountains, trees, prairie

I imagined

It was difficult to watch

something being taken

but what

exactly

And in the foreground on the surface of the lake

an ellipsis of buffleheads

travelling in the opposite direction

Yesterday was the warmest December day in recorded history

It was the night before

the night before

your surgery

and we walked out along the railyard in light jackets

saying nothing

about the chatter of idling locomotives

or what the surgeon would take from you

for your own protection

with a fibre-optic cable system

and a scalpel

your fallopian tubes illuminated by halogen

How do we protect ourselves

against the future? It sounds ridiculous

against the future

You'd always wanted your own babies

Ellipsis

I'd never seen a golden eagle

the colour of a locomotive

like the one that darkened the water over the little train of ducks

that day in Sunnybrae

her talons

yellow brackets

her mottled bronze wings

calculating

gravity

I don't know how to be against something

so immense

shadow water

shadows

water

The warm air felt so good and terrifying at the same time

It was hard

to believe. It felt mistaken

as if we were in the wrong

dream. To prepare

for your surgery, the hospital sent you instructions

for bringing home your baby

Ellipses

It was hard to believe

such a mistake could be made. It was too dark

walking the streets

to see the shale and limestone faces

of the surrounding

mountains

just their heavy presence

over which the subtropical jet stream rolled

romantic, bewildered

like us

through the glitter of chickweed in the alley

the red blinking eye of the radio cell tower

in the darkness above the lake

railyard floodlights

Sweet air sweet air

what's your freight, what's your cargo

Someday

two days from now

the nurse will wheel you

across the glass vestibule of the hospital

through the sensor-

activated sliding doors

into the proper cold of a December evening

where I'm waiting

by the black electric car

to receive you

This is the future

so much

yet undecided

The ellipses of coloured lights

outlining buildings all over the city

the injured and saved

the newly born and forever altered

trading places

on the concrete apron

so many doors opening and closing

Doxa

For once I was permitted

a meadow

where everyone was disguised

as ghosts

beneath sheets

of heavy snow. The whole world was brilliant

white

except the waves

of blue shadow

washing across the uneven snow

the tarnished

antennae of grasses

above the ice crust. I held up my phone

and doxxed the meadow

the screen populating with plant names

and the names of animals

one intelligence

arising, I thought, from another intelligence

itself arising

from something

I didn't yet understand

as intelligent. It was a mistake

Reality is always virtual

I thought, looking beyond the screen

at the meadow

that is not mine but is a made place. A voice in the mind

connected the pixels on the screen

to the pixels of snow

only one of which was a perfect illusion

In the sky, the sun worked

its last weak angle

of argument

across the meadow

the waves of blue decaying

to blue pools

the wildrye ablaze with signal

I surveilled the scene

with my imagination: inside all matter

tiny particles spun

in and out

of existence

Lightform, winterseed, *everlasting omen of what is*

forgive me. I had the sensation

of free will

I had ice cleats on the bottom of my feet

Resolution

See the filament of wildrye

in snow

its yellow noonday light

and blue shadow

against ice

a white-gold brightness scattering

like seeds

across the field

Remember the old spirits

from the deep earth

burning

orange-blue

and unseen

in the electrical room

The past is never closer

than in the heart

of winter

To love the future

without you

you resolve yourself

its heat

its mystery

its change

what you will never see

what you will never see again

Return Enter

for Zac Whyte

Then we double-spaced the trees

and between the lines

streamed

trails of light

rushing away from us

We chose select all

and in the blue glow

saw the cinnamon bear

you were riding in your blue hospital gown, going nowhere

you wanted to go. You held

his fur and a secret

white stone

you called *oblivion*

its read-only memory, its hard drive

its astonishment

This is what it's like

you said re: rebooting

your glitchy heartbeat

every few weeks

about the propofol and ketamine protocol

the joules they burn into you

what you prepare for

with your eyes-closed, noise-cancelling black omega

headphones

what you hold onto

Elsewhere

someone was making lunch for our children

in what passes

in this realm for solid matter

Elsewhere

we were kids again shooting hoops in the driveway

like an analogy for everything

that moves

through us

the stone in your hand

that meant

as long as you held it

you'd return

as you were, continuous with yourself

renewed but the same, the same, always the same

Delete the stone

Type a new scene in the driveway

kids drinking lemonade

the colour of treelight

a basketball spinning backwards in a high arc

toward its negative shape

the houses double-spaced, then double-spaced, then double-spaced

until only openness

rushes at you. Delete the stone

I said in your headphones

but your fingers were only streaming

trails of light

with no mass, no touch. Inside you

something was buffering

buffering

Pine Marten

for Xilo

The teenagers kept changing

their names

and pronouns

an event

in the coding

from within which something ambiguous

blurry and free

could be seen

emerging. From the very beginning

we didn't know you

by your name

only the familiar myriad reflections

glinting

in your sinewy, water animal

body, our own code

recoded

our creed, our oath. At the lakeshore, late winter

a pine marten

the colour of late winter snow

kept popping up

like a new window

within which could be glimpsed

the lakeshore

white

with dark markings

When the motion-activated marten reloaded

in a new spot

it watched us like a camera

searchlight eyes

panning rapidly across our shadowed bodies

for danger

safety. What does it mean

to be seen

to be affirmed and confirmed

as what you are

the whole schoolyard of boys surrounding you

like ice

in a dream

of thaw. When the marten slipped off

its winter-made lake coat

and blinked itself

out of sight, it transformed

into what it always was

the lake

the lakeshore

the mountains brimming with lake colour

the deep watery sky

Kopenhagener Str. 15

for Maria

The sky came suddenly close

like a friend

with a disclosure

of rain

Then, just as suddenly, retreat

drawback

unburdened distance

across the bright vaulted sky

And in the aftermath

chestnut blossoms on cobblestone

puddlelight

in the Mauerpark

finchsong

Each window in your courtyard

showing its own film

of blue sky, clouds

Some things are so poetic

they can't be

invented. How in the Hauptbahnhof

when the train gathers

to a full stop

you feel yourself

drop

into the sunk bolt perfect rhyme

of your body

as if the difference

between what you perceive

as your mind

and your mind were revealed

for an instant

and distance healed

Two Prisms

In the days before

the invasion

at the last edge

of winter

the Japanese maple

blushed

along its thinnest branches

its silver bark

taking on a crimson undertone

the tiny cut-ruby buds

brimming

with returning light

old as war older. Every time

I had thoughts

I had only more thoughts. In the canyon

the river

was two rivers

one frozen heavy opaque

time's memory

dissolving

and the other excited light

running clear

pure verb

pure flicker and rush

beneath the ice

Real Things

If violets bloom in August
the books say
that means a death is coming
Or a pandemic

You can tell a violet from bladderwort
by the fine ink markings
in the lowest petal
a few dark marks
where you split your lip open

Some things are more
Real than real

My friend hated himself
so much he wanted to die
Then he hated himself more

for wanting to die

for how his children would suffer

He called me the other evening

after you and I had climbed trails

and decommissioned roads

through light rain

and you'd put your finger

right next to the tiny

alpine bitterroot

growing in the middle

of the mountain path

after we'd walked

through meadows

of strawberry

chocolate lily

larkspur

after you named for me

the tangled line of blue clematis

and I'd shown you

the calypso orchids

on the side of the ridge

purplish and erect

all turned in one direction

their large white lips

their filaments

of golden hair

He said his sister killed herself

by accident

went downstairs

on Christmas Day

to drink herself to sleep

because of something

he didn't name

and I didn't name

but that we both knew

she could only escape

in the dreamless sleep

of alcohol. He was scared

of his sister, he told me

and for her, the intensity

of her emotions

how alike they were

She didn't want to die

he said, she said that

I don't want to die

The word calypso

derives from Ancient Greek

to cover or hide

He found her

the next afternoon

wrapped in white bedsheets

face purple

hair golden still

a few feet

from where he'd been

reading

to his nine-month-old

daughter

I'm showing you the orchid

but I'm thinking

of the violets

we'd seen that day

in the mountains

even though it was not August

and a death had already come

blue, yellow, white

You only get to be you

Death is *Real*

How the tiny bitterroot

is no bigger

than the tip

of your finger

How everywhere

violets bloom

At Smoothing Stones Bridge

June has come to

the bridge-

head. Turned one way

it's onslaught. Turned

the other

abandonment

Watermark day moon

even the outer atmosphere

at full pool

The creek channel

livestreaming

bank failures, rate change

Along the oxbow

blue bubbles of polyester tents

where people live

No more austerity

only floods of gold

buttercup

I face you

your fury, your passion

your gravity

Sky heavily bandaged

with cloud

above the unstaunched creek

The missing woman

and her dog won't be found

in poetry

Soldiers in the old poems

don't care

about flowers or freshets

Come down

from the high mountain

rough water, mind

People built this crossing

over the tumult

for future people

O to be swept off

by a torrential self-emptying

love

Beneath the bridge

of heaven, the relentless flowing banner

of heaven

Notes & Acknowledgements

I respectfully acknowledge the Syilx Okanagan people on whose traditional and unceded territory I wrote these poems.

Earlier versions of several poems first appeared in the following publications: *Social Alternatives* (AUS), *32 Poems* (US), *Penny Dreadful* (IRE), *Event* (CAN), *Filling Station* (CAN), *Canada and Beyond* (SPN) and *Best Canadian Poetry* (CAN).

"Heat Dome" quotes the opening lines of Samuel Taylor Coleridge's "Kubla Kahn."

"Atmospheric Moon River" was written for the Sharon Thesen Lecture at the University of British Columbia Okanagan in April 2022. It appeared as a limited-edition chapbook with Anstruther Press. Thank you to Jim Johnstone. The poem repurposes the early 16th-century lyric "Westron Wynde" as transcribed by Charles Frey. The phrase "tomorrow sex will be good again" comes from Michel Foucault via Katherine Angel. The term "psychic excess" comes from Judith Butler. I won't explain the joke about William Butler Yeats.

"Doxa" quotes, misquotes and references Robert Duncan's "Often I Am Permitted to Return to a Meadow."

"Pine Marten" borrows the line "ice in a dream of thaw" from Seamus Heaney's poem "The Rescue."

"Real Things" was written for Xilo, when they were twelve, and for Will Johnson.

Thank you to Sarah Rose Nordgren and her online writing community for inspiration and feedback on early drafts of several of these poems. Thank you to Maria Alexopoulos, Xiaoxuan Huang, Harold Rhenisch, Natalie Rice and Rob Taylor for the conversations about many things including these poems.

Thank you to Myron Campbell, again, for the cover.

Thank you to Silas White and everyone at Nightwood Editions for the many years of collaboration.

I gratefully acknowledge the support of the British Columbia Arts Council and the University of British Columbia.

About the Author

Matt Rader is an award-winning author of six volumes of poetry, a collection of stories and a book of nonfiction. His previous book of poems, *Ghosthawk* (2021), was shortlisted for the Dorothy Livesay Poetry Prize. He teaches Creative Writing at the University of British Columbia Okanagan and lives in Kelowna, BC.

Photo by Maria Alexopoulos

Lite Reading

What does a good future look like?

I asked the plum tree

as I steadied myself

on the aluminum stepladder. In its bare branches

the tree held open a few choice pages

of daylight for me to read. That's what it asks here, I said

but the plum knew that passage

from memory

being a natural, as it were, in the literature

of water and heat. It's wild, I said

opening and closing

the pruning shears like a clapperboard

how much it takes

to extract and alloy these metals

meaning the blades of the shears, the pin

pinning them together

meaning the steps of the stepladder

From where I stood

I could tell the tree

was ignoring me, reading

ahead to where the light would gather

years from now

Good answer, I thought there in the lines of the tree

where, if I stood still

long enough, even I could feel

the late autumn sun

inscribing my body with energy